Help Me JESUS

Compiled by
Marian Bennett

488

STANDARD PUBLISHING
Cincinnati, Ohio   2273

What's It All About?

"Jesus Christ, who are You, what have You sacrificed?" A popular musical echoes the question of the day, "Who is Jesus?"

For two thousand years people have pondered the question. The answer affects each of us. We must know who He is before we know how to react to Him. We need to know the answer now. Are our lives to be meaningful or futile, happy or unhappy? What's it all about?

Who did Jesus say He is?

Throughout Jesus' ministry, He was dropping hints to reveal His identity. He talked of light, a vine, a judge, bread, a door, truth, life.

Who is He? Open your eyes to the truth. Listen to what He has to say.

Library of Congress Catalog Card No. 72-82084

© 1972
The STANDARD PUBLISHING Company
Cincinnati, Ohio
Printed in U.S.A.

Contents

Daybreak, the Son is Shining

"Again therefore Jesus spake unto them, saying, I am the light of the world: he that followeth me shall not walk in the darkness, but shall have the light of life" (John 8:12, A.S.V.).

Who turned out the lights? It's dark down here. People are bumping into each other. No one can see beyond the end of his nose. If only someone would turn on a light! This seems to be a pretty good place, basically, if it just weren't so dark!

Right on! We live in a dark place. The Word teaches that this world is under the dominion of the power of darkness. (Read Colossians 1:13.)

Good news is here, however. The Son has come up. "I am the light of the world." Is this just an arrogant claim, the words of a braggart? For a man to claim this would be boasting. But that's the key; Jesus wasn't a mere man.

Jesus was at the temple in Jerusalem. It was "big-party" time, the festival of Tabernacles. (Read John 7:2, 14.)

On the first night of the festival there was a ceremony called "The Illumination of the Temple." Four huge candelabra were prepared in the court of the temple. When it grew dark, the candles were lit. They sent such a blaze of light throughout Jerusalem that every courtyard in the city was lit with their brilliance. All night long, the greatest, wisest, holiest men in Israel danced before the Lord and sang songs of joy and praise to God while the people watched.

The light was symbolic of God's past guidance of the Jews through the wilderness and their hope for deliverance from their present darkness of foreign oppression. The ceremony was a meaningful experience for the Jews.

Then Jesus appears. "I am the light of the world!" Not just the light of this temple. Not just light for this evening. Light for all mankind, for all time. In Him there is guidance for all men, hope for all men.

Even in this dark world, then, there is a way to know where you are going and how to get there. The directions were revealed in the God-man, Jesus.

"But ye, brethren, are not in darkness, that that day should overtake you as a thief. Ye are all the children of light, and the children of the day" (1 Thessalonians 5:4, 5).

Words from the Word: Matthew 5:14; John 3:19; Acts 26:18.

Prayer thoughts: Praise God for sending the Light of the world. Ask for discipline to study the truth He revealed. Ask for His guidance in everyday decisions. P.T.L.

—Tom Smith

To Be Satisfied, Eat the Bread of Life

"And Jesus said unto them, I am the bread of life: he that cometh to me shall never hunger; and he that believeth on me shall never thirst" (John 6:35).

Bob had it made, so everyone thought. He had plenty of money, a trust fund set up for his college and summer travel, good looks, plenty of available chicks, terrific build, ability in all the major sports. But Bob said, "I'm empty. I'm not satisfied with my life."

Everyone seeks to be satisfied, content with life. It is a feeling of being complete, at peace, a feeling of knowing you've done all that is expected of you. The loose ends are tied, the unfinished business finished, the differences resolved. The restless soul is at rest and the hungry heart is filled.

What does Jesus mean when He calls himself the "bread of life"? In that day, bread was the great sustainer of life, the essential part of the diet. Christ is referring to something far more than mere physical existence when He speaks of life, however. He is talking about relationship with God—knowing God through an intimate, personal relationship of trust, obedience, and love. That's life. Someone said, "Christianity is not a religion, but a relationship."

Jesus is the way we get this life. He is our sustenance. He holds the unlimited supply of life essentials. A person dies when he stops eating physical food. So it is when there is no consumption of spiritual food.

When one is genuinely hooked on the Lord, eating the bread of life, he can no longer get hungry or thirsty. He is satisfied. He knows for sure. "I'm OK." God loves me.

The great thing about God's love is that it frees us to be ourselves. When we know, "God loves me just as I am," we no longer try to be something we aren't. We don't have to be superpopular, pretty, handsome, athletic, musically inclined, or any of those things the world uses to judge. We give up every kind of stupid competition there is in this world.

The Lord doesn't look on the outside (see 1 Samuel 16:7). He looks on the inside. All He asks is that we let Him love us, and love Him in return. When we know we are loved by God and by His people, the church, when we find real friends in the family of God, when we find a place to give and to help others, we will be satisfied.

Trying to find satisfaction? Forget the drugs; forget the ego trips in the popularity bag; forget trying to be the big man at school; forget yourself.

Feast on the Bread of life.

Jesus satisfies.

Words from the Word: Luke 15:11-24; Ephesians 2:19-22; John 6:25-35.

Prayer thoughts: Ask the Lord to help you know He loves you. Ask Him to help you understand His Word. Rejoice in knowing you are beautiful. Be satisfied, give the glory to Jesus.

—Tom Smith

Jesus Is Boss

"Ye call me Master and Lord: and ye say well; for so I am" (John 13:13).

Everyone wants a saviour, but very few want a lord. Many come to Jesus because they want to be forgiven, or want to become a church member. But how many accept Jesus as both Saviour and Lord?

The lives of some church people cause many in the world to reject Christianity. Many churchmen in this country think you don't have to really "lay your life on the line" to be a Christian. Just sit through one or two services a week, pay the preacher a dollar, and you've arrived. Someone has propagated a spineless, uncommitted Christianity. Uncommitted Christians? What a gross contradiction of terms!

Look closely at Peter's sermon on the Day of Pentecost: "Therefore let all the house of Israel know assuredly, that God hath made that same Jesus, whom ye have crucified, both Lord and Christ" (Acts 2:36).

What does it mean to say, "Jesus is my Lord"? It means "Jesus is boss." To acknowledge Jesus as Lord is to recognize His authority over all of life. Not just Sunday morning, but Lord of our social life, vocational plans, recreation, material possessions, school life. To let Jesus be Lord is to bring all of life under the beautiful canopy of His leadership.

Each decision, in every sphere of life, should be preceded by, "What does Jesus want me to do?"

The church has to start getting tough. The church must be made up of people willing to let Jesus rule their lives, willing to die for the truth of the gospel. Christians must be willing to stand up against the forces of darkness of racism, prejudice, and greed.

We must be willing to have the guts to overcome our nervousness and witness, share with those around us. "Hey, brother, here is a New Testament. Have you ever really considered Jesus?"

Think of the apostle Paul. He was repeatedly beaten, thrown in jail, stoned, shipwrecked, deserted by his friends, called a heretic by church leaders. Yet he had the guts to keep going, to keep loving. "I know whom I have believed." Paul knew who was boss.

We must be willing to let the Lord's church be a family, not afraid to love one another and be loved. At all times we must remember, "Jesus is boss of the whole enterprise."

Our ultimate goal will be "that every tongue should confess that Jesus Christ is Lord, to the glory of God the Father" (Philippians 2:11).

Words from the Word: John 13:12-20; Ephesians 1:2; Revelation 19:16; Philippians 2:9-11.

Prayer thoughts: Praise Jesus that He is Lord of the universe. Ask for the power to overcome self to the place where Jesus can truly be your Lord. P.T.L.
—Tom Smith

Hook Into the Vine

"I am the vine, ye are the branches: He that abideth in me, and I in him, the same bringeth forth much fruit: for without me ye can do nothing" (John 15:5).

"I am the true vine." Sound strange?

Here's this fellow sitting in an upper room with a small band of followers. He is saying, "Peace I leave with you, my peace I give unto you: not as the world giveth, give I unto you."

Well, I can buy that. He is supposedly a religious teacher and those types are always concerned with peace. But what about this vine stuff? What did Jesus mean when He called himself the "true vine"?

The place to begin is with the common vine we all know about. Think back to botany. What is the function of the vine in the whole life of the plant? Simply this, the vine is the supply line between the source of essential elements and the fruit-bearing agents. The vine transports water, nitrogen, phosphorous, potassium, and other important nutrients. It goes from the vine to the branches and leaves where the photosynthesis process takes place, and fruit is produced. Cut the vine and the plant dies, because the essentials of life are no longer available.

Are you getting the picture? Jesus was saying, "I am the supply line between you and the essentials of life found in God."

The essentials for real living—truth, purpose, meaning, answers, forgiveness, new birth—are being supplied to you through Jesus. Try to get them on your own and you will fail. A branch can't produce fruit without being hooked into the vine.

Also, when Jesus said He was the true vine He was shouting at Israel, the Jewish people. The vine was used as a symbol on the gateway to their temple. To the Jews the vine symbolized their destiny as the source of truth about God.

Jesus was revealing that a new vine, the true vine, had arrived on the scene. This vine would truly give a fruitful life.

Note the reason for Christ's coming: "I am come that they might have life, and that they might have it more abundantly" (John 10:10).

In Galatians 5, the Holy Spirit lists the style of life, the fruit enjoyed by those hooked into the vine: love, joy, peace, longsuffering, gentleness, goodness, faith, meekness, and temperance.

Draw of the essentials of life that are available at the feet of Jesus. Jesus gives fruitful, abundant life.

Words from the Word: John 15:1-14; Romans 6:11; Galatians 5:22-26.

Prayer thoughts: Give thanks to God that He sent His Son to this planet to give us the truth upon which joyous life can be built. Pray that you might bring forth fruit for God.

—Tom Smith

The Door to Happiness

"I am the door: by me if any man enter in, he shall be saved, and shall go in and out, and find pasture" (John 10:9).

James Taylor and Carol King were appearing in Chicago. This was the concert everyone had been waiting for. Tickets had been sold out long ago. However, a few people were selling tickets, at exorbitant prices, for friends who decided at the last minute not to come. Everyone was frantically trying to find a ticket. Then the concert started. The doors were closed. To add to the frustration, those on the outside could hear the muffled roar of the sound systems. They couldn't get in. There was no available entrance.

Jesus called himself the "door." What did **He** mean?

In Christ's day, sheep were collected into sheep-folds at night. A hillside sheepfold was just an open space enclosed by a wall. There was an opening through which the sheep came in and went out, but no door of any kind. At night the shepherd lay down across the opening, and no sheep could get out, nor could a predator get in. The shepherd was the door. There was no access to the sheepfold except through him.

There had been many false messiahs and self-appointed leaders before Jesus' time who had worked havoc with the flock. The scribes and Pharisees had just given an illustration of this by throwing out of the synagogue the poor beggar whom Jesus had cured.

The phrase used in verse ten for "having it more abundantly" is the Greek phrase that means to have a surplus, a superabundance of a thing. To be a follower of Jesus, to really know Him, is to have a superabundance of life.

Life is so beautiful when you are inside—inside the kingdom of God. The way to get in is through Jesus, the door. Don't worry. He never runs out of tickets. He will give you one at the door. Believe and obey.

See you on the inside. The music is beautiful.

Words from the Word: Matthew 7:13, 14; Acts 8:35-39; John 10:7-10.

Prayer thoughts: Ask God to help you to be obedient to His Son. Pray for the guidance as you study the Bible. Rejoice in the Lord.

—Tom Smith

One Way

"Jesus saith unto him, I am the way, the truth, and the life: no man cometh unto the Father, but by me" (John 14:6).

"One way, one way, one way," chanted the crowd in Cincinnati's Fountain Square one spring day. Crowds have taken up the chant all over North America and around the world.

The One Way sign, the fist with a raised index finger, has become the new symbol of Christendom. Not only do "Jesus freaks" use it, but also straights, ministers, Sunday-school superintendents, Christians everywhere. It is a great symbol because it is based in Scripture.

"I am the way." That is a powerful statement to us. Consider what it meant to the Jew who heard it for the first time. The Jews talked a lot about the way in which men must walk and the "ways" of

God. God said to Moses: "Ye shall not turn aside to the right hand or to the left. Ye shall walk in all the ways which the Lord your God hath commanded you" (Deuteronomy 5:32, 33).

The psalmist's prayer was: "Teach me thy way, O Lord" (Psalm 27:11). Jewish priests and scholars sometimes spent their entire lives studying to become experts on the ways of God.

Then up walks Jesus and says, "I am the way." Simple as that. Can you imagine how it must have blown their minds?

What did Jesus mean? William Barclay illustrates this by having us imagine we are in a strange town asking for directions. Suppose someone says, "Take the first street to the right, and the second to the left. Cross the square and go past the church and take the third road off the right." In all probability we will be lost before we get across the square. But suppose the person we ask says, "Come, I'll take you there." In that case the person to us is the way, and we cannot miss it.

This is precisely what Jesus has done for us. We know the way to God because we have the perfect road map in the Scriptures. But even more, we have the presence of Christ, the Holy Spirit, to take us by the hand and lead us to joy in the presence of the Father.

We must be willing to be led.

Words from the Word: John 14:1-6, 16, 17; Psalm 1.

Prayer thoughts: Ask the Lord to lead you through His Word and by His Spirit. Enjoy the trip.
—Tom Smith

Here Comes the Judge

"For as the Father hath life in himself; so hath he given to the Son to have life in himself; and hath given him authority to execute judgment also, because he is the Son of man" (John 5:26, 27).

"Here comes the judge, here comes the judge, order in the court, 'cause here comes the judge." Right. These were the lyrics to a song on the pop charts a short while ago. Such would have been appropriate to announce the approach of Jesus two thousand years ago.

The "Judge" was another title the Lord used to identify himself.

Too often we think of religion as merely being that which tells us what we can't do. The New Testament speaks more about what man should do than what he should not. Christianity is a positive statement of faith, not negative.

We must remember, however, that we are responsible for our thoughts and actions. We will someday stand before the Lord and be required to "give account of ourselves."

That can sound scary. But lest these scary feelings grow into terror, we should look closely at who will be doing the judging, for in Him there is comfort and hope.

Man's judging is usually unjust. Our judgments are often blinded by our prejudices, intolerance, self-righteousness, conceit, and ignorance. It is only a man whose heart is pure and whose motives are completely unmixed who can judge another man, and that is to say that no man can judge any other man.

On the other hand, the judgment of God is based on the character of God and is perfect. God is holy and He knows the standards by which all men and all things must be judged. God is perfectly loving and His judgment is delivered in charity. God has full knowledge, the knowledge of a man's mind, his hassles, his handicaps, his temptations.

Jesus was the Son of man. He came to earth to live among men. He had the same desires and feelings that we have. He fought the same hassles, was tempted by the same adversary who tempts us. He was the sympathetic Jesus.

Jesus is the Son of God. He has the perfect mind of God. Certainly He will be able to judge us with the same perfect justice shown by God.

Do not be afraid.

Accept the truth and obey it. Love the Lord and all His children and you shall be counted in the "resurrection of life."

Words from the Word: John 5:19-30; Acts 10:40-42; 2 Timothy 4:8; James 5:9.

Prayer thoughts: Recognize Jesus as the just, loving Judge of the universe. Ask for the Spirit's aid to help you be more obedient to His Word.

—Tom Smith

The Riddle

"For I am persuaded, that neither death, nor life, nor angels, nor principalities, nor powers, nor things present, nor things to come, nor height, nor depth, nor any other creature, shall be able to separate us from the love of God, which is in Christ Jesus our Lord" (Romans 8:38, 39).

Do you like riddles? Try this one:

You didn't join it voluntarily, but you can never give up your membership.

Sometimes you can't live with it, but then you can't live without it either.

You want the protection and security it offers, yet sometimes you want to get away from it.

You love it and you feel hostile toward it, and sometimes you have both feelings at the same time.

Have you guessed the answer? The family. Think about it. Isn't this the way you feel about your family?

All families have problems. No family is perfect. That's the way it is; that's the way it should be.

When God established the family unit, He knew what He was doing. The family is just the place for finding out about God's love, about self, and love for others.

God's love knows no bounds. Read the Scripture quotation again. Recall John 3:16. Read 1 John 3: 1, 2; 4:10-21. The family is the best place for learning to receive God's love. In family relationships, people know us—know our faults, our bad habits, our disagreeable ways—yet still love us. That's the way it is with God. God loves us as we are. We sin, we stumble, we make mistakes, but God continues to love us. We do not earn the love of our family, nor do we earn the love of God. It is given freely. The love of parents, brothers, and sisters is limited. It is an imperfect love, but it does point to Him whose love knows no limits, whose love is perfect.

In the family we not only learn to receive love, we learn to give love. Just being loved helps us to love others. You might say the family is a sort of laboratory for learning, growing, and developing relationships with others. It is the best place for learning to receive and give love.

Prayer thoughts: Thank God for His limitless love for you. Thank Him for your family. Ask Him to help you use your family as a laboratory for learning to receive and give love.

—Ruth Odor

What the World Needs Now

"If a man say, I love God, and hateth his brother, he is a liar: for he that loveth not his brother whom he hath seen, how can he love God whom he hath not seen? And this commandment have we from him, That he who loveth God love his brother also" (1 John 4:20, 21).

Read Matthew 5:43-48; Romans 13:8-10.

Love is a word we hear and see a lot these days— in songs, books, commercials, on posters, in movies, everywhere! People are saying we need more love in the world, more love in our lives. A lot of people use the word love when they really mean sex, but I know that's a mistake. That's not the kind of love the world needs.

Years ago, Jesus, You were talking about—and living—the kind of love we need today. It's a special kind of love that most people don't understand, because they don't know You. They feel a need for Your love, but they don't know that You're the source of it. So it's part of Your plan for us that we show Your love to others.

The hang-up for a lot of us is not understanding that Your love isn't so much an emotion (a love feeling) as an act of will (a love action). It's not so often expressed in love words, embraces, and nearness, as in kindness, helpful deeds, forgiveness, and goodwill. That's how it's possible to love an enemy— someone who's unloving or uninterested. You still can do loving things for him and keep an attitude of goodwill toward him. Sometimes it takes an act of will to love a brother, too—a friend or fellow Christian!

This is a time when we're being forced to look inside ourselves for traces of ethnic and racial prejudice. This is another place where Your love comes in, Lord. Paul said the only way we can be sure of fulfilling all Your commands concerning our relationships with others is to love our neighbor as ourselves, to have the same concern for his welfare as we have for our own.

And Jesus, You told us in Your parable of the good Samaritan that our love, like Yours, mustn't set up artificial boundaries of race, background, creed, or social standing. Our neighbor is whoever needs us. And so many people need us; or rather, need Your love demonstrated in us.

Prayer thoughts: Jesus, fill me so full of Your love that I just can't help loving others out of the overflow. Show me who my neighbor is—the welfare mother on the other side of town, the black child in the ghetto school, the teen-ager up the street who's messing with drugs. Then show me the best way to love them so they'll know it's really You who is the source of love. Amen.

—Donna McQuilkin

God? Who's He?

"Philip saith unto him, Lord, shew us the Father, and it sufficeth us. Jesus saith unto him, Have I been so long time with you, and yet hast thou not known me, Philip? he that hath seen me hath seen the Father; and how sayest thou then, Shew us the Father?" (John 14:8, 9).

Additional Scriptures: Isaiah 37:16; Jeremiah 10:10; Hebrews 1:1-4.

The teen-age years are packed full of group activities and good times. Though most of these activities are fun, they sometimes lead to things that are wrong. Probably many in the group would refuse to do such things as individuals, but in order to gain group acceptance, they go along with the crowd. If someone does have the courage to take a stand against the wrong by saying that his belief in God will not allow such actions, the others are likely to say, "God? Who's He, man?"

Who is God? This is a question that deserves an answer. There is much said in the name of God today, and the name of God is much said in the wrong way. Those using the name of God seldom know much about Him. Even though you think you know Him, there is always more to learn.

Philip was close to Jesus. He had heard Him teach, seen the miracles He had performed, heard the answers He had given the Jewish leaders. Yet, Philip asked Jesus, "Show us the Father." The answer Jesus gave Philip is helpful for us, today, as we seek to understand more about God. Jesus said, "He that hath seen me hath seen the Father." Jesus didn't transport Philip into some mystical realm where he could see God firsthand. Rather, Jesus told him to study the facts available to him by observing Jesus' own life.

Many today desire a supernatural revelation of some kind to reveal the personality of God. The words of Jesus still stand. To know who God is and what He is like, go to the Son. Jesus taught and lived according to the truth of God. His thoughts, His words, His actions, His desires, His motives were pure. His love was pure and unlimited just as the Father's love is. Just as God is holy, so was the life of His Son on earth.

The next time someone asks who God is, answer him, "He's the One Christ came to reveal unto man." Even if the question is asked in sarcasm, an answer like that will open a door for effective witnessing.

Prayer thoughts: Pray for courage to be able to withstand group pressures and live for Jesus. Pray for a closer walk with Jesus that you may know God more intimately. Pray for opportunities to share your faith with others. Pray that others may see God-like qualities in you.

—Mark McGilvrey

What's the Secret of Happiness?

Jesus said, "These things have I spoken unto you, that my joy might remain in you, and that your joy might be full" (John 15:11).

Check into Philippians 4:6-8, too.

"How can I be happy?" This is the big question for most people.

Some try to find happiness in *doing,* and keep themselves busy at everything from tiddlywinks to snowmobiling. Others try to be happy through *having,* and they strive for good grades, recognition in athletics, or status as a musician or performer.

Entertainment is the magic road for some. Television, the movies, or novels bring them into a plastic fantasy world where they live thrilling lives of excitement. This way they don't have to face up to drab reality.

But these things are all counterfeit. Happiness is not something outside—it is inside! Happiness does not depend upon the circumstances life brings to us but on the attitude we bring to those circumstances!

The secret to happiness is this: The happiest person is the one who has the happiest attitude! Simple as that.

God's Word teaches us to have a happy attitude toward ourselves. We are created by almighty God. We have infinite value to Him. The God of this universe actually loves us. Loves *us*!

We are also told to have a happy attitude toward others. Jesus' commandment, "Love thy neighbour," leads to happiness. Jealousy, envy, resentment, and hatred all result in our unhappiness.

Our attitude toward God should promote happiness when we realize that He provided a means of salvation for our sins. God sent His Son to rescue us from sin—from unhappiness and misery, too.

Do your thoughts make you happy or unhappy? We have little control over the flashes that pass quickly through our minds, but we do have control over the long-term outlook on life that is uniquely ours.

In Philippians 4:6-8, Paul told the Philippian Christians the kind of thoughts that would lead to happiness. Herein is the secret.

Prayer thoughts: God, do You want me to be a happier person? Why am I so unhappy at times? Help me see what is wrong with me—no, help me trust in You more—and be a happier Christian.

—Rod Huron

Between Sundays

"Having your behavior seemly among the Gentiles; that, wherein they speak against you as evil-doers, they may by your good works, which they behold, glorify God in the day of visitation" (1 Peter 2:12, A.S.V.).

Read 1 Timothy 4:11-16; Matthew 5:13-16.

People know what you are by your actions. It is wonderful to be busy in church activities—teaching a class, being president of the youth group, playing the piano for the Teen Department, being class secretary, singing in the choir. You are a real ball of fire—on Sunday, that is.

What are you doing between Sundays, though? Do you sort of take off your Christianity as you take off your good clothes? Do you set your Christian ideals on a shelf until they are needed again? Are you as willing to help at home through the week as when you are at church? Or, do others think of you as only a "Sunday Christian"?

If those who see you on Sundays could see you during the week, would they recognize you? Or, let's turn it around—if those seeing you during the week saw you at church on Sundays, would they know it was the same person?

A teen-ager had been trying for some time to get his neighbors to go to church with him. They finally agreed to go with him the following Sunday. But Saturday night, the boy had a group of teens from the church come to his house for a party. They stayed so late and made so much noise that the older couple couldn't sleep. The boy could never quite figure out why his neighbors didn't go to church with him the next day.

Working for the Lord on Sunday is great, but don't destroy that witness by your actions during the week. Being a Christian is a full-time job. It includes consideration for others, tolerance, forgiveness, respect, helpfulness, honesty, and love.

Ask yourself this question: If all the members of my church were to live the way I do through the week, what kind of congregation would we have? Would we be winning others to Christ? How would the community feel toward God? Be honest with yourself.

You know, there may be among your friends one person who will never come to Christ unless you witness to him. Maybe a minister, a Sunday-school teacher, an adult could never reach him. He is waiting to see Christ in your life—all week long.

Prayer thoughts: Pray that your actions may be a witness for Christ. Ask for strength to remain faithful each day of your life.

—Donna Goodrich

My Parents Don't Understand Me

©HVAS

"Bear ye one another's burdens, and so fulfil the law of Christ" (Galatians 6:2).

Read Colossians 3:20, 21.

Lord, my parents just don't understand me. Like last night—

I wanted to use the family car to take the fellows to the game over in Centerville. Dad said no. Wouldn't let me take the car. Man, was I ever let down! Like what else is there to do on a Friday night?

Come to think of it, Lord, I never stopped to look at it from Dad's point of view. I guess he wasn't being selfish about the car after all. He was really thinking of me, wasn't he—my safety, my protection. He cares about me. Guess it was a long and risky trip. A lot of things could have happened.

Lord, I just never stop to think about why Mom or Dad speak or act as they do. I forget that they may be tired or worried. You know, it must be rough being a parent and having all that responsibility, and having to make all those decisions, and worrying about your kids and everything.

I forget, too, that my parents had parents, and sometimes they act the way they do because their parents acted the same way.

I forget that parents aren't perfect. And, Lord, I'm surely glad they aren't, for it would be mighty rough living with perfect people.

Lord, the next time I complain that my parents don't understand me, help me to realize that it could be the other way 'round—maybe I don't understand my parents. Maybe I haven't tried to understand them.

Help me, Lord, to look at things from their point of view—at least once in a while—at least to try. Help me to learn to talk to Mom and Dad as I talk to You. And, Lord, lead us all to a greater understanding of one another.

Prayer thoughts: Pray for better understanding of self; for better understanding of your parents; and for God's help in trying to figure out why your parents act as they do in given situations.

—Ruth Odor

Who Is Gullible?

"For thus saith the Lord that created the heavens; God himself that formed the earth and made it; he hath established it, he created it not in vain, he formed it to be inhabited: I am the Lord; and there is none else" (Isaiah 45:18).

Additional Scriptures: Genesis 1:1; Job 38; John 1:1-10; Hebrews 11:1-3.

Anyone who is willing to believe without reservation that God created the heavens and the earth is said to be gullible in many circles today. Yet it seems as if the shoe is on the other foot, and those who hold to the theory of evolution are gullible.

There is nothing scientific about evolution. For a study to be scientific, it is necessary that a certain procedure be strictly followed: (1) the problem must be defined; (2) all the data that relates to the problem must be gathered; (3) a hypothesis must be formed; (4) experiments must be performed to prove or disprove the hypothesis; (5) the experiment must be repeated and observed to assure that the same results follow each time; (6) the data from the experiment must be recorded and organized; and (7) conclusions may be drawn.

Obviously, the origin of the universe cannot be studied by this method. It is absolutely impossible to take the fourth, fifth, and sixth steps; thus, origination is outside the scope of science. Those who believe that evolution is scientific are, therefore, gullible. They have been fooled into regarding a philosophic system as a scientific system.

Those who hold to evolution are also gullible in believing that they do not have a god in their explanation of the origin of the earth. When an evolutionist is backed into a corner on a given issue, he appeals to his god of infinite time and the difficulty is resolved. Given an infinite amount of time anything can happen, he claims. Rather than being more rational than the Bible, this system is absurd. Every time reason breaks down, the undefined factor is interjected into the formula, allowing the evolutionist to manipulate it any way he likes. Instead of a logical system based on set rules, evolution is an illogical system based on that which is undefinable.

The Bible proves through prophesy that it is a supernatural book. Through the miracles of Jesus, God proved that He is in control of the earth and all of its elements. In every area that it is possible to test the truth of the Bible through archaeology, it has been found to be true. The Biblical account of creation does not present any loose ends that must be tied up by appealing to the undefined. Not a single fact of the Biblical account is contradicted by true science. Who is gullible, the Christian or the evolutionist?

Prayer thoughts: Thank God for the revelation He has provided in the book of Genesis that answers our questions about creation. Pray for understanding and strength to stand up to any ridicule that may come as a result of taking a firm stand on creation by God. Pray that man will respect the world as a creation of God and not pollute or misuse it.

—Mark McGilvrey

Pressure, Problems, and Tension

"Thou wilt keep him in perfect peace, whose mind is stayed on thee: because he trusteth in thee. Trust ye in the Lord for ever: for in the Lord Jehovah is everlasting strength" (Isaiah 26:3, 4).

Check into Psalm 37:3-5, too.

PSALM 23—TODAY'S VERSION

The clock is my master; I shall hurry on. I have much to do that is urgent. No peace can I find for a moment.

My stereo plays in my bedroom, and dad wants it turned down "Right now!" Report cards are coming on Monday, and I know this will mean a big row.

My parents and family beset me. Can they not leave me be for one day? I resent their commandments and orders, and wish they'd stay out of my way.

I cannot walk through these dark shadows. The pressure is more than is fair. Surely no one encounters the load that I carry. Must I dwell in this madness forever?

Ever feel like that, or worse? What are you to do when things pile up? An explosion doesn't do much good because usually all you have left after an explosion is pieces. The aftermath can be worse than the cause.

Should you quit? Pout? Whine? Bellyache? Take a look at the way Jesus handled His problems. He had enemies that were trying to kill Him—and they finally succeeded. His friends were not much help, and often misunderstood Him. People crowded around Him so much He couldn't find time to eat! All the while He was carrying the responsibility of rescuing the world from sin.

How did He do it? He did it in two ways: (1) He organized His priorities, and didn't waste a lot of time on things that didn't really matter. (2) He left everything in the hands of God. Even in Gethsemane, when the pressure was intense, He prayed, "Thy will be done."

How can you put your life more in the hands of God? Are there any problem situations you can eliminate? How can you do a better job of coping with the ones you cannot eliminate?

Prayer thoughts: Explain to God the problems you have and ask His help in sorting them out and getting it all back together.

—Rod Huron

The Membership Role

"Now therefore ye are no more strangers and foreigners, but fellowcitizens with the saints, and of the household of God; and are built upon the foundation of the apostles and prophets, Jesus Christ himself being the chief corner stone" (Ephesians 2: 19, 20).

Read Acts 4:32-35; Ephesians 2:19-22; 4:4-6.

Dropout. There's a word with a heavy sound, and one we hear a lot these days. Dropouts from society, from school, from the establishment, from church. Some of the kids I've grown up with in Bible school and church have dropped out along the way. It's a sad fact that many teen-agers leave the church, but why? If you asked them, they'd probably say they got bored with the same old lessons; tired of hearing the same old don'ts; couldn't understand the preacher's sermons; the church isn't relevant today; their parents always made them go but now they can decide for themselves.

Some of those things may be true sometimes, but I have a hunch they're mostly excuses. I think the real reason must go deeper. I mean, what about all the rest of us who stuck it out and even managed to grow a little, in spite of an uninteresting teacher or an occasional boring sermon?

I wonder if the real reason they slipped away was that they really didn't know what the church is all about. Maybe they didn't even know Jesus, the head of the church. Their names were on the book, but they didn't belong to Jesus.

If that's the real reason why they dropped out, the next question has to be, How? How could they be a part of our fellowship for weeks, months, years, and still be "strangers and foreigners"? How could they share in our singspirations, class discussions, wiener roasts, and calling programs, and still not be of one heart and soul with us? How could they sit through dozens of Bible lessons and sermons and still not know enough to become a member of the one body in Christ?

How? We let it happen because we failed to show them that the church is more than beach parties and work days, rallies and revivals. It's a Person, and we're His people. He's the head, and we're the members. We're His eyes, to look for those who need Him. We're His hands, to share; we're His feet, to run; His tongue, to speak; His heart, to love.

Prayer thoughts: Help me, Jesus, to know what it really means to be a member of Your body, the church. Help me to live my faith and to love my friends so neither I nor they will slip away, drop out, and lose You. Amen.

—Donna McQuilkin

First-String Christians

"Wherefore seeing we also are compassed about with so great a cloud of witnesses, let us lay aside every weight, and the sin which doth so easily beset us, and let us run with patience the race that is set before us" (Hebrews 12:1).

Additional Scriptures: 1 Corinthians 9:24-27; 2 Timothy 4:1-8; Hebrews 12:1-6.

Not many people think of Christianity as an active sport. Most Christians seem to think that God wants His people to be passive spectators. Many have the idea that they are meeting the Lord's requirements for Christian living by simply attending worship services. Christianity thus becomes a mere spectator sport.

The minister, elders, deacons, choir members, and Bible-school teachers are considered to be the players in the Sunday morning "game." They are judged to be skillful or unskillful on the basis of the performance that they stage each week. If these star players are agile and quick in their mental moves, they stand a good chance of attracting large crowds to watch them play. When the crowds grow large enough to build a beautiful building to watch their stars in, the church is labeled a success. In fact, this view of Christianity is so prevalent today that many prominent church leaders automatically assume that it is the proper one. Preachers and Bible-school teachers encourage their people to become fans of God. This is a step in the right direction for many drowsy spectators, but it is only a small step.

The Bible does not picture Christianity as a spectator sport, but as an action sport. Christians are not to arise from the waters of baptism to take their seat in the bleachers and cheer the church stars on to victory. The Bible says that Christians are to get into the game and play as though the eternal destiny of the world depended on them, because it does. In the track meet of life every Christian is called to carry God's colors.

You go into all the world (Mark 16:15). *You* are the light of the world (Matthew 5:14). *You* are a chosen generation (1 Peter 2:9).

All of God's people have skills that can be utilized in the meet, but many have never left the locker room. Some Christians literally grow old and die attending locker-room pep talks and strategy meetings without ever telling anyone about Christ and without making any changes in their own lives. If the church is going to be successful in the contest with Satan, all the players must be in top condition and ready to battle the enemy with all their strength. There is no place on God's team for spectators or lazy, locker-room loungers. God calls all of us to be first-string athletes.

Prayer thoughts: Thank God for the challenge of Christian living that demands the best that lies within man. Pray for courage and determination to carry the gospel to the lost. Pray that God will use you to make Christians aware that God wants them to be first-string Christians.

—Mark McGilvrey

True or False?

"If any would not work, neither should he eat" (2 Thessalonians 3:10).

Read Matthew 19:16-22, 27-29; Mark 10:35-40.

True or false? You can have privileges without responsibilities. False. Privileges mean responsibilities, and there's no way around it.

Today we may be led to think differently. All around us we see free love, demonstrations against authority, and disregard for rules and laws. It seems many young people want unrestricted liberty, freedom to do as they please. They do not find freedom this way, however. The more privileges one takes, or is given, the more responsibility he must assume.

Kim's mother gives her a clothing allowance and lets her shop in town alone on Saturday. Kim is thrilled with all this freedom. Aha! Now she can buy what she pleases! Then she realizes that with this new freedom comes a new responsibility. She is responsible for the money entrusted to her. She has to make choices she has not made before.

Jerry's dad lets him have the family car for the first time, a long-awaited privilege for Jerry. But as Jerry sails down the highway, suddenly he thinks of the responsibilities that are now his. He is responsible for the car, for himself, for the other occupants of the car, and, to some degree, for the other drivers on the road. Now, HE, not someone else, is responsible.

Accepting responsibility is good. It means that

you are growing up. The more responsible one becomes, the more privileges he enjoys. If Kim handles her money wisely and makes good choices, she will enjoy more independence in other things, too. If Jerry uses common sense in his driving, and takes care of the family car, he will get to use it more often.

In our Christian lives the same thing is true. Everyone wants the promise of an eternity free from work, sickness, trouble, and heartache. That's Utopia! How many are willing to do their part—take the responsibility of living and working for Jesus here on earth—to enjoy the privilege of heaven? After becoming Christians, we tend to sit back and watch others assume the responsibilities in the Lord's kingdom, and yet we expect to receive the same reward, or privileges.

God has given you a free will. You can choose to accept responsibilities and then enjoy the resulting privileges, or you can let others carry the burdens and forget your reward. The choice is yours.

Prayer thoughts: Thank God for making us free to choose for ourselves; for giving us Christ in whom we find forgiveness of sin; for Christ in whom there is true freedom. Ask for guidance in use of privileges and assuming of responsibilities.

—Ruth Odor

It Takes a Dope to Try Some

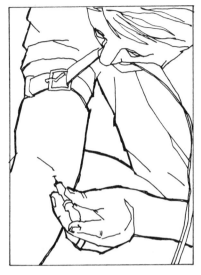

"Know ye not that your body is the temple of the Holy Ghost which is in you, which ye have of God, and ye are not your own? For ye are bought with a price: therefore glorify God in your body, and in your spirit, which are God's" (1 Corinthians 6:19, 20).

Check into Hebrews 13:20, 21, too.

You know the words: Horse. Grass. Pot. Snow. Speedball. STP (Serenity, Tranquility, Peace). Hard stuff. Mesc. Lid. Bag.

And the words surrounding the big scene: Narc. Connection. Speed freak. Bad trip. Wiped out. Pusher. Bust. Turn on. Cold turkey. Loaded. Getting the Glow. Stoned. Habit. Dealer.

And the technical ones: Psychedelic. Cannabis. Hallucinogen. D-lysergic acid diethylamide. Addiction. Methedrine. Psychological dependency. Amphetamine. Syringe. Rehabilitation.

Someone has probably warned you of the legal penalties. Thirty-one states provide a minimum of two years in prison for a first conviction of possession of marijuana, and forty-four states have maximum penalties ranging from five years to life for the same offense.

Doubtless you have been tuned into the mountain of information being compiled as research is done into the relationship between drug usage and chromosome breakage, damage to the kidneys, liver, and central nervous system, and the extent of lasting psychological imbalance.

So what?

None of this may be enough to keep you from turning on. All these words mean nothing when somebody lays it right on.

What about this word? JESUS.

Do you think He went to the cross so you could trip out? Don't you know you're putting Him down? Do you think He lied when He promised to give you joy, so you have to find "joy" somewhere else?

Get high on Jesus, and stay high! No blackouts with Jesus!

Prayer thoughts: Tell Jesus how you feel about drugs. Tell Him who is trying to get you into the action. Explain to Jesus that you want to make the scene with Him, and ask Him to help you split the drug scene completely.

—Rod Huron

How Do You Feel About Love?

"He that loveth not knoweth not God; for God is love. In this was manifested the love of God toward us, because that God sent his only begotten Son into the world, that we might live through him" (1 John 4:8, 9).

Additional Scriptures: Romans 5:7-11; Ephesians 2:4-7; 1 John 3:1.

How do you feel about love? That sounds like a line straight from a romantic novel or movie, but in reality it has serious meaning. John writes in his first epistle, "God is love." Since John equates God with genuine love, to ask how you feel about love is to ask how you feel about God. Now, there's something to think about.

Your attitude toward God is very important because attitudes shape actions, and actions fix destinies. If you have a feeling of love toward God, your actions will be an expression of that love as you seek to please God. On the other hand, if you harbor an attitude of animosity or even hatred toward God, that too will be expressed in your deeds. The actions of obedience and love done to please God become the basis of salvation for the person who loves God. The hateful, spiteful deeds of the person who does not love God become the basis for his condemnation. It seems, then, that everyone needs to check up on his attitudes toward God.

There are several reasons to love God. For one thing, God created man to be the ruler of the earth. That fact alone should cause us to love God, but that's just the start. God created man as a companion. That really makes the true God easier to love than the gods of the heathen who are said to have created man as slaves to do their dirty work.

God is pure. Here again, the living God is easier to love than the pagan gods whose lives were characterized by wickedness. God sustains us by providing for our physical needs. God is always there when He is needed. God never deceives man. God knows everything and will guide His creatures, if they will let Him. Obviously, God is perfect. There is nothing to dislike about Him at all.

God is not only easy to love because of His perfection, however. He is also easy to love because He loved us first. Even though man sinned against God and deserved to die, He sent His only Son into the world to suffer and die for us that we might live eternally. A love like that demands a responsive love. God's love cannot be taken lightly because it cost Him the life of His own Son. Now, how do you feel about love?

Prayer thoughts: Pray for strength to love everyone. Pray that you will have the proper attitude toward mankind and God. Thank God for His righteous love for us. Thank God that He created us to be His children, not His slaves.

—Mark McGilvrey

It's Your Move

"Ye are our epistle written in our hearts, known and read of all men: forasmuch as ye are manifestly declared to be the epistle of Christ ministered by us, written not with ink, but with the Spirit of the living God; not in tables of stone, but in fleshy tables of the heart" (2 Corinthians 3:2, 3).

Judy came from a non-Christian home. She attended a university and became a kindergarten teacher. Realizing that something was lacking in her life, she began searching. She found Christ and became a Christian.

Judy enrolled in Bible college to add knowledge of Christ to her secular education. Her family had disowned her when she became a Christian. For years they would have nothing to do with her. Judy kept an attitude of love rather than bitterness, and quietly and steadily witnessed for her Lord. Eventually she was able to lead her entire family to Christ.

Lord, can my family see You in me? Not very often, I'm afraid.

This is where witnessing begins, doesn't it? At home. My family should be able to see You in me— in my attitude, in my words, in my actions. That's easier said than done, Lord.

Perhaps my witness would be stronger if I spent more time with You, Lord, thinking of You, being aware of Your presence, talking to You in prayer. I need to become more acquainted with Your Son through Matthew, Mark, Luke, and John.

When I am deciding how to react to a situation, I ought to ask, "What would Jesus do?" "What would Jesus say if He were here?" "Would Jesus be willing to go with me to this place and do what I will be doing?"

Perhaps my greatest witness, Lord, is my joy in belonging to You. I am Your child. I wear the name of Your Son.

"It is no longer I that live, but Christ liveth in me: and that life which I now live in the flesh I live in faith, the faith which is in the Son of God, who loved me, and gave himself up for me" (Galatians 2:20, A.S.V.).

Prayer thoughts: Think of your own family. Pray for their particular needs. Take a look at yourself. Are you a good witness to your family for Christ? Ask God to help you find ways to witness daily.

—Ruth Odor

A Friend Indeed!

"A man that hath friends must shew himself friendly: and there is a friend that sticketh closer than a brother" (Proverbs 18:24).

Read Proverbs 17:9, 17; 22:24, 25; John 15:12-15.

Sometimes I catch myself looking with envy at the kids who seem to be popular with everyone at school. What magic quality do they have that makes kids follow them around like the Pied Piper, eager for just a smile of recognition or a casual "hello"? Are they superskilled at the art of making friends, or do they just have a few more brains, a little more money and class than the rest of us?

Everyone needs to have friends. Not all of us can walk away with the popularity prize, but we all need a few friends we can talk to and be close to. Friends don't just happen; you have to be a good friend to have good friends. It doesn't hurt to take a few lessons from the Friend of friends.

Lesson one is love. The greatest expression of love is to sacrifice your life for your friends, if necessary. Jesus did this. But chances are we won't be required to. Instead, we have to love by living, which might be even harder! We have to overlook the faults of others, be forgiving when we think we've been betrayed, be generous and helpful.

Lesson two is trust. That means being honest and truthful, loyal to a friend in trouble, and most important, it means knowing when to keep your mouth shut! Solomon said that when friends have a falling out, the really loving thing to do is keep quiet about it. To repeat it to someone else and keep harping on it will cause a break that might never be healed.

It's important to be a little choosy about the kind of friends we have, too. A friend who'd try to turn us away from the Lord certainly isn't worth having. Solomon warns that we should steer clear of people who can't control their temper. To learn the ways of undisciplined friends is to put our souls in danger.

Everyone needs friends, and the greatest Friend is Jesus. He's promised to make us His friends if we obey His commands. As His friends, we can talk freely to Him, share His love, trust Him. He's already proved His love by laying down His life for us. What kind of friend am I to Him?

Prayer thoughts: Dear Jesus, I thank You for the many good friends I have to share my life. Help me to be a good friend to them. It's great to be able to share You with my friends, too. May we always take You with us. Amen.

—Donna McQuilkin

Hold It!

"Whatsoever ye do, do all to the glory of God" (1 Corinthians 10:31).

Read James 3:1-14.

A minister was speaking to a group of teen-agers. His topic was "Hold Your Tongue." He asked the teens to try to hold their tongues with their fingers. Try it. Hard, isn't it? In fact, it is practically impossible.

Not only is it hard to hold your slippery tongue with your fingers, it is equally difficult to keep from saying the wrong things. Too often we "release our mouth before our mind is in gear."

Many of us belong to the "talk now, think later"

club. So what's wrong with that? I say what I want. I don't care what others think about me. Is that so? How about what others think of your God? Could you possibly be giving the wrong impression to those who are not in the body of Christ? Many times, all they know of God is what they see in your life and conversation. That makes your tongue a lot more important part of your body, doesn't it?

Think back over the last conversation you had with your friends. How many people did you talk about? Did you speak only what you knew to be true, or did you pass along a rumor or two you heard from someone? Although you told the truth, was it something that needed to be told? Even the truth hurts at times.

If you want your witness to count for the Lord, hold your tongue. Don't be involved in petty gossip, spreading rumors about everyone you know. You'll have a hard time convincing anyone that you belong to Christ. Rather, make your conversation a testimony for God and His Son. Let them speak through you.

Prayer thoughts: Ask God to help you in your conversation that all you speak may be "to the glory of God."

—Donna Goodrich

My Will Versus God's Will

"Jesus saith unto them, My meat is to do the will of him that sent me, and to finish his work" (John 4:34).

Additional Scriptures: Psalms 143:10-12; Matthew 6:9-15; John 4:27-34.

We often feel that to get the most out of life we must exercise our freedom of will. The radio blares out songs encouraging us to exercise our freedom of will for our own pleasure—"I've Gotta Be Me," "It's My Life and I'll Do What I Want."

Everywhere we go people are saying, "Do your own thing." This constant encouragement to allow self-will to rule our lives causes many problems. Our freedom of will gets us into trouble when we choose to satisfy our own desires rather than do the will of God. In the contest between our personal will and God's will, our will often wins out but heartbreak and ruined lives may be the result.

Jesus shows us the way to real pleasure in life. Christ was so delighted at the conversion of the woman at the well that it totally overcame His hunger for physical food. That's real joy when you can forget an empty, growling stomach! Jesus experienced this joy when He carried out His Father's will. In fact, Jesus calls this His meat. Just as a thick slab of roast beef can supply our bodies with refreshment, strength, and enjoyment, a healthy portion of time spent in doing God's will can satisfy our spirits.

True happiness and peace come through doing God's will. A spirit fed on the candy, pop, ice cream, potato chips, popcorn, pie, and cake of self-will can expect to grow fat and weak. This condition leads to an unhappy and restless life. A spirit fed on the lean meat of God's will becomes fit and strong. How do you want to feed your spirit? Man's will can lead to a broken heart and a weak spirit; God's will leads to a happy heart and a strong spirit.

Prayer thoughts: Thank God for giving you freedom of will. Pray for strength to resist the constant temptation to misuse your free will. Ask for the strength of character to surrender your will to God's will. Pray for the blessings of peace and happiness that come through putting God's will first.

—Mark McGilvrey

My Brother's Brother

"For none of us liveth to himself, and no man dieth to himself" (Romans 14:7).

Read Colossians 3:12-14; 1 Peter 4:8.

Lord, I just have to be honest with You. The way I feel about my brothers and sisters—well—

Lord, they're just first-class stinkers, that's all. They bug me! The younger ones are pests. They're always hanging around, in the way, wanting to tag along, bothering me when I want to be alone, using my possessions.

My older sister is a plain snob. Thinks she's a V.I.P., bossy, always telling me what to do, ducking out on jobs, getting around Mom and Dad. Say—I wonder if I've treated the younger ones the same way at times?

If I'm going to grow as a Christian, guess I'll have to learn to get along with them, won't I? Maybe if I worked out a plan—like:

Step 1. Look for their good qualities instead of their bad ones. Come to think of it, there are a few. Sis sometimes explains to Mom why I do some of the things I do. And she lets me in on what to expect of certain teachers and classes at school. And the little ones. It's really great when they look up to me. "That's my brother, Bill," they say.

Step 2. Try to understand them. Put myself in their place.

Step 3. Listen. Give them a chance to be heard. What they have to say just might be important.

Step 4. Work out a plan for sharing things, such as the baseball bat or the badminton set.

Step 5. Talk things over with Mom and Dad. When I don't think I'm being treated fairly, I guess I should just tell them about it. I suppose I should keep in mind that the family is made up of individuals, and parents show their love to each child in a different way.

Well, that should get me started in the right direction, shouldn't it, Lord?

And by the way, thanks for them—brothers and sisters, and Mom and Dad. It's nice to have people who care about you and count on you.

Prayer thoughts: Use the above meditation to help you formulate your own prayer concerning your brothers and sisters. Ask for guidance in getting along with one another.

—Ruth Odor

Honest, Now, Is That the Truth?

"Thou shalt not bear false witness against thy neighbor" (Exodus 20:16).

Check into Ephesians 4:14, 15, 21-25, too.

Charlie Brown and friend were sitting under a tree and "friend" was talking about how wishy-washy Charlie is. Finally C. B. says, "The truth is just as wishy-washy as I am!"

Charlie must have been watching too many TV commercials, with their flagrant disregard for the truth, or maybe he had read too many newspaper ads.

Our knowledge of applied psychology often leads to disregard for the truth. Coach says, "Hey! You'll make a great team! Best bunch of freshmen I've ever seen!" and all the while he is thinking, "Whew! We'll be lucky to make seventh place with this outfit!"

Though there have always been those who played fast and loose with the truth, God has always demanded truth. When God asked Adam and Eve, "Where art thou?" He wanted the truth! When God asked Cain, "Where is Abel thy brother?" He wanted the truth!

Jesus always spoke the truth. He did so with gentleness and grace, but it was always the truth. In the upper room He said, "I am the way, *the truth,* and the life."

So important is honesty that God has decreed all liars shall have their part in the lake of fire (Revelation 21:8).

Dishonesty eats at our character like a cancer. The observation, "To be a good liar one needs a good memory," points out the fact that one lie leads to another, then to another, until finally the liar would not recognize the truth if he were to see it.

Deceit, cheating, lying, and stealing are all first cousins, and are close relatives of the devil. Even that cool pastime, shoplifting, is rotten in the eyes of God.

Behind the mask you put up before others, what is the truth about yourself? What about your relationship with God? How honest are you before the One who knows the secrets of every heart?

Does telling the truth give you the right to say unkind things about someone else? Would "speaking the truth in love" ever mean telling an untruth?

Prayer thoughts: Ask God to help you to be honest with Him, with yourself, and with others.

—Rod Huron

Doing God's Thing

"I have written unto you, young men, because ye are strong, and the word of God abideth in you, and ye have overcome the evil one. Love not the world, neither the things that are in the world" (1 John 2:14, 15, A.S.V.).

Read Romans 12:2; James 1:27; 1 John 2:14-17.

Suppose John were alive today. What are the chances he'd write a letter like this to me? "I have written to you, _____ _____, because you are strong, and the Word of God lives in you, and you have overcome Satan." Could he say about me, "You are strong"?

I'd like to be a strong person, but it's hard! Every day I run into pressures designed to make me weak. The kids at school expect me to carbon-copy their clothes, musical tastes, language, and opinions. Oh, it's not usually a conscious pressure—that's what makes it so hard to resist! It just happens, before you know it. And when I conform, I feel a sort of strength because we're together. But is this really being strong? Is this the kind of strength that will help me overcome Satan?

Some of my teachers demand conformity too. I don't always agree with a teacher's conclusions, but I dutifully parrot them back on exams so I won't get graded down. That's not being strong! I've got a lot to learn, but thinking for myself is part of learning.

Even my parents expect me to pattern myself after them in a lot of ways. That's not all bad, of course.

I love and respect my family, and I'm especially thankful for my heritage of Christian faith. But I can't be like them in every way. I have to be me!

Then there are all those unseen, unnoticed ways the world tries to mold my thoughts and my life. "Buy this product; go to this college; enter this profession; believe this philosopher; achieve these goals!"

I need to pay more attention to John's warning: "Don't center your love on things in the world, or God will get shut out. After all, the world is going to disappear, but God is forever." And James: "Don't get polluted by the world." And Paul: "Don't let the world squeeze you into its mold; instead let God change you from the inside out."

Prayer thoughts: Lord, I want to fit the pattern You've made for me, not the pattern of the world. Strengthen Your love in me so there's no room in my heart for the things of the world. Let Your Word live in me so I'll be strong in You. Amen.

—Donna McQuilkin

What Do I Owe God?

"Every good gift and every perfect gift is from above, and cometh down from the Father of lights, with whom is no variableness, neither shadow of turning" (James 1:17).

Additional Scriptures: Psalm 24:1-6; 1 Corinthians 6:20; 2 Thessalonians 2:13-17.

Have you ever caught yourself wondering why you should serve God? Has the question, "What do I owe God?" ever entered into your mind? Perhaps you have been spending quite a bit of your time lately doing church work and feel as though God owes you something. When you begin to think your account with God is paid up or that God may even owe you some benefits for your hard work for Him, it is time to take a look at the balance sheet.

James 1:17 gives us the total of God's gifts to man. It says that all the good things in life are supplied by God. That is a mighty large total. Like a large sum of money, however, it tends to be meaningless until it is broken down to understandable dimensions.

First of all, let's see what every good gift includes in the physical realm. It certainly includes all the beautiful scenery that exists on the earth. Man has not fashioned the world into beautiful mountain peaks capped with snow, rolling plains, and mighty oceans. No human process is responsible for the grandeur of the Grand Canyon. No plumbing shop put together the dynamic water display at Niagara Falls.

The gifts of God to man also include the rich resources of our earth that provide us with delicious food, fine homes, fuel for heat in the winter, and metal for machines that make our lives more pleasant. Our oceans, lakes, beaches, ski slopes, and forests that provide us with great times of recreation are gifts from God. God has blessed us with the sound of beautiful music.

God has also given us wonderful spiritual gifts. In creating man in his own image, He has given us the capacity for love. God has given us the ability to reason and to use our minds to make our world a better place in which to live. He has given the whole earth to man as his kingdom and made it subject to his desires. God has given man the ability to know right from wrong. He has placed within us the freedom of choice that we might not be bound as slaves to our Creator. God has given us immortality. Through God's ultimate gift of Christ, man can live forever in peace and comfort.

The books are poorly balanced. God has given us everything we have and has made us everything we are. No matter how much we may work for Him we cannot outgive Him or even come close to equaling His gifts to us. What do you owe God? Everything.

Prayer thoughts: Thank God for our wonderful world and all its beauty. Pray that we will learn to subdue it properly and to stop polluting our environment. Thank God for Christ, the best gift that He could give. Pray that you will learn to live as though you owe God everything.

—Mark McGilvrey

Lord, Am I a Chimney?

"Know ye not that ye are the temple of God, and that the Spirit of God dwelleth in you? If any man defile the temple of God, him shall God destroy; for the temple of God is holy, which temple ye are" (1 Corinthians 3:16, 17).

Check into 2 Corinthians 7:1, too.

Do you realize that our laws permit you to carry a three-inch cylinder of poison so deadly that one drop injected into the bloodstream can kill?

The story begins with a fire (gets rid of weeds and pests that ruin things if they can). After the fire, work up the soil and plant the seed. Put the chemicals on and keep the weeds out. Top it, cut it, and hang it.

When the price is right, down it comes for the auction, then to the factory, where it will be sorted, sanitized, shredded, and boxed in 20's. From here it goes to the store where you can buy it, unwrap it, and start another fire—just a little one this time— on one end.

The other end goes in your mouth, and you suck. That's it.

It's called smoking, and it's great. So "they" say. "Old Moldbags—For Those Who Want Taste." "Try Crumbalms—They Satisfy."

And why not smoke? Lots of people do it. Besides, whoever heard of a seventeen-year-old with lung cancer? Go ahead and smoke.

Aren't you polluting Somebody's temple? Is that life really yours to use up?

C'mon now, are you going to let that little bitty god tell you that you have to do something, that you *must* have a smoke, that you *will bow down* to its all-powerful demands?

Are you going to let that little white cylinder run your life?

What would Jesus say?

Prayer thoughts: Jesus—want a cigarette? I'm embarrassed I asked You. Sorry. I shouldn't smoke, I know, but all the kids do and they'll make fun of me if I don't. I can't stand to be made fun of. Do You know what it's like? You do? They made fun of You? How did You stand it? Did You give in? You didn't?

Jesus—help me not to give in, either. Don't let this thing make me its slave. Help me, Jesus.

—Rod Huron

Generation Gap

"Now I beseech you, brethren, by the name of our Lord Jesus Christ, that ye all speak the same thing, and that there be no divisions among you; but that ye be perfectly joined together in the same mind and in the same judgment" (1 Corinthians 1:10).

Read Amos 3:3.

Big talk these days—the generation gap. Sounds as if youth and adults live in two different worlds with an uncrossable gulf between. Is there such a thing as a generation gap? Perhaps there doesn't have to be one unless we make it.

Oh, sure, adults don't dig long hair, groovy clothes, pop art, or rock records. And teen-agers don't dig Bing Crosby, Renoir, or Guy Lombardo. But this doesn't mean that there can be no understanding, no communication.

When you get down to the nitty-gritty of troubles between adults and youth, the reasons seem to boil down to two: (1) we—both sides, that is—are too selfish to want to understand, and (2) too lazy to make the effort. Often adults are too busy going about their lives to take time to consider the feelings and the problems of youth. And youth fail to take the time and effort to try to understand adults—their hang-ups, their problems, their concerns.

Each needs to remember that it's a two-way deal. And each needs to take time to try to understand the other, to "be still and know." Stop, be quiet, think, listen, and know—know self and the reasons why we feel and act as we do, know the other person and why he feels and acts as he does.

And once we try this "be still and know," let's go on to communicate with one another, to sit down and talk over problems, difficulties, misunderstandings, desires, needs. This doesn't mean that there will be no conflict. It can mean peace and happy co-existence.

The Christian family—Christian adults and youth —are way out in front in the business of avoiding this thing called a generation gap, for they are united in a common purpose, a common goal. There is respect for one another, confidence in one another, respect for individuality. There is time, for one's time belongs to Christ. There is effort to understand and to communicate, for in Christ's love others become more important than self.

Sure, there are still two generations—still all the differences in dress, appearance, language, likes and dislikes, but the things that matter—our aim, our purpose, our chief love—know no differences, make no gaps.

Prayer thoughts: Pray to learn to "be still and know." Ask for guidance in understanding and communicating, for unity in Christ's love.

—Ruth Odor

I Have My Rights!

"I know, and am persuaded by the Lord Jesus, that there is nothing unclean of itself: . . . For the kingdom of God is not meat and drink; but righteousness, and peace, and joy in the Holy Ghost" (Romans 14:14, 17).

Read Romans 14:2-13; Colossians 2:16-23.

We hear a lot about rights these days: individual rights, civil rights, constitutional rights. The rights we have guaranteed in our constitution and laws are very important and very precious to us. If someone tries to violate them, we don't just sit and take it; we stand up for our rights!

I hadn't thought much about it before, but Christians have some important individual rights given to them in their constitution, the Bible. These passages from Paul's letters to the Romans and the Colossians mention some of those rights.

A Christian has the right to have his own opinions and follow his conscience about certain matters not mentioned specifically in the Scriptures. Paul gave the example of food and drink, because this was an issue for the Gentile Christians. Some of them felt they shouldn't eat or drink anything that had been offered to idols before it was sold in the marketplace. Others felt that there was no harm in this, since Christians weren't bound by Jewish laws and, after all, God had created these as well as other meats.

Paul agreed that there was nothing evil in the food itself, but if someone thought it was wrong to eat it, then for him it was wrong. However, he shouldn't try to force his opinion on someone else and judge him if he didn't agree, just as no one was to judge that man.

It's not hard to see how this can apply to me! I wonder how often I've violated someone's "Christian rights." I know some kids at school who don't believe in doing certain things that I consider all right. In other cases, the situation's reversed. They're Christians, and they have the right to their opinions about these things, just as I have a right to mine. But I wonder if I haven't judged them, secretly anyway, branding them "narrow-minded" or "liberal" just because they don't agree with me! I have no right to make those kinds of judgments.

On the other hand, I have a right to stay free in Christ from rules and practices made up by men. The rules may seem to make these men more holy or humble than others, but they really have nothing to do with faith.

It seems, then, that a person's Christian rights are at least as important and precious as his civil rights.

Prayer thoughts: Lord Jesus, I thank you that we are free in You to be ruled by the law of love. Help me remember not to judge others who may not share my opinions. Help me to respect the rights of others as well as to guard my own rights. Amen.

—Donna McQuilkin

Hello... Who Is Speaking?

"If any man among you seem to be religious, and bridleth not his tongue, but deceiveth his own heart, this man's religion is vain" (James 1:26).

Check into Matthew 26:69-75, too.

Profanity is one of the most difficult of all habits to break. Ask Simon Peter. Jesus had completely changed Simon during their three years together, and Simon had been transformed from a rough fisherman into a consecrated disciple.

Yet, during the crucial hours when Jesus was on trial, we are shocked to see Peter cursing and swearing that he does not even know Jesus!

It was a surprise to Peter, too. Earlier that same evening he had promised Jesus that he would never deny Him, that he would die first. In spite of all his high resolves, Peter lapsed back into his old ways again, the cursing, swearing fisherman.

Profanity is a surprising thing. We are shocked when that first swear word slips out. But, you know, the next one comes easier, and it isn't long before it becomes a habit.

What's so wrong with swearing, anyway?

Profanity exhibits a basic lack of self-control. The profane person is not controlled by the will of God. Even though you may not habitually use profane speech, when you have that burst of temper that brings the forbidden words to your lips, it should be quite clear that, for that moment at least, God is not in control.

Analyze profanity. Notice the references to God,

to Jesus Christ, to Hell, and being condemned or damned to Hell, or to the natural but personal function of the human body, such as elimination or sexual activity.

In every case there is coupled disrespect for God or persons, or both, and contempt for the one being cursed.

Can you imagine Jesus telling shady stories to the disciples around the campfire at night, or angrily swearing at some poor leper who was bothering Him? It is blasphemy to even consider, yet when we do it, Jesus does it—if we are Christians, for He is to be living in us.

Prayer thoughts: Open up to God those moments of anger when you lost your temper and your tongue. Ask God to help you control your speech, so you will speak for Christ, never in a way that shames Him.

—Rod Huron

All Together Now

"If two of you shall agree on earth as touching any thing that they shall ask, it shall be done for them of my Father which is in heaven. For where two or three are gathered together in my name, there am I in the midst of them" (Matthew 18:19, 20).

Read Philippians 4:4-7; James 5:13-16; Mark 11:22-26.

This time you spend with God each day is really paying off, isn't it? Everyone needs a time each day to spend alone with God. Each family needs a time for the family members to be together with God. Family devotions can do a lot for you and your family, but you'll have to try it to find out.

If your family doesn't have devotions, why can't you be the one to suggest it? Set a time—at breakfast, before or after the evening meal, or just before bedtime.

Try a three-part plan: (1) listening to God; (2) talking together; (3) talking to God. Read a chapter from one of the Gospels, or an epistle, or a Psalm. Follow a plan; don't just read the page where the Book falls open. Different members of the family may take turns reading. Use one of the newer versions: Amplified Bible, Phillips' translation, Today's English Version, The Living Bible, The New English Bible. Younger children may read (when their turn comes) from a Bible reader (such as Basic Bible Readers, available in Primer through Grade Four).

Discuss the Scripture as it relates to life. Ask questions. Bring up problems. Tell some good things or bad things about the day. Give each one a chance to talk. Listen to what the others have to say.

Then talk things over with God. You may want to have a prayer circle as you do at camp, standing in a circle, holding crossed hands, and each praying in turn.

Try conversational prayer. This is simply conversation directed to God as well as to each other. In conversational prayer, we become aware of the other person, what he says, what he means, and how he feels; we stay on the same subject (by taking turns, listening, speaking, agreeing, giving thanks); and we try to keep in tune by maintaining interest in the current subject instead of introducing a new one too quickly. As we pray we recognize the presence of Christ; we say "Thank You, Lord"; we ask for help for ourselves and for others.

Getting started with family devotions may be a little difficult at first. Finding a time that suits everyone is not easy. People are often shy about reading or praying before others. If you try it, however, you'll find that there's nothing quite so special as your family and God meeting together.

Prayer thoughts: If your family already has devotions together, ask God how you can take part more effectively. If your family does not have devotions, ask Him to give you the courage to suggest the idea.

—Ruth Odor

I Protest!

"Rebellion is as the sin of witchcraft, and stubbornness is as iniquity and idolatry. Because thou hast rejected the word of the Lord, he hath also rejected thee" (1 Samuel 15:23).

Read Numbers 20:1-13; Deuteronomy 21:18-21; 1 Samuel 15:1-23.

Many adults have labeled today's teens a rebellious generation. And I guess we are rebellious in a lot of ways, but not all of them are bad. A certain amount of self-assertion is part of growing up. It's our way of testing out our brains, our reasoning powers. We have to try out some of those principles we've been taught and make them our own.

Some of the things teens today are rebelling against aren't worth hanging on to, either, like apathy, materialism, prejudice, hypocrisy, discrimination. Trouble is, most of those things are pretty deep-rooted in our society. Kids find out that one or two impassioned speeches or good deeds don't do a whole lot toward ridding the world of some evil. Then they lose their cool and start rebelling against everything! And, of course, they get into trouble and are disillusioned with what they thought was right. We need to realize that it may take a lifetime to get rid of apathy or prejudice just in ourselves!

It's one thing to rebel against the things that aren't right in this world, and it's quite another to have a rebellious spirit—to rebel against all authority except oneself. That means a person is rebelling against God, too, and He takes that pretty seriously!

For example, when the children of Israel reached the desert of Zin on their journey from Egypt to Canaan, they began to complain. They griped to Moses and Aaron about the lack of food and water and other bad conditions, instead of being grateful to God for freeing them from slavery. Moses and Aaron, instead of acting like the leaders they were supposed to be, disobeyed God. As punishment for their rebellion, God told Moses and Aaron that they wouldn't be allowed to enter Canaan.

When God sent King Saul against the Amalekites, His orders were to destroy every living thing, man and beast. But the people wanted to spare the king as hostage and the best of the livestock as spoil, and Saul went along with them. He rationalized it by saying they'd sacrifice the animals to God. God wants obedience more than sacrifice, however, and Saul was punished by having his kingdom taken from him.

Prayer thoughts: Lord, use me as a rebel against the evil in the world, but may I never rebel against Your command and authority. May I never grieve my parents with a rebellious spirit. In Jesus' name, amen.

—Donna McQuilkin

Aliens in a Hostile World

"I was glad when they said unto me, Let us go into the house of the Lord" (Psalm 122:1).

Additional Scriptures: Psalm 107:6-8; John 4:23; Hebrews 10:23-27; 11:13-16.

A Christian is an alien in a hostile world. He cannot feel at home in a sinful world. How hard it is to live this way, always on guard so that Satan won't cause him to stumble and fall into sin. The strain is terrific, but God has provided the Christian with a haven of rest. There's one place where the weary Christian can feel at home, where he can be refreshed and strengthened. That place is the worship service of the church.

Worship is the means that God has provided to keep us on the road to heaven. At times we are tempted to stop traveling the straight and narrow paths of righteousness and follow the comfortable, broad road that leads to destruction. When the smog of the polluted world causes us to lose sight of our goal, then we need to come before God's throne in worship.

Through singing songs of praise, hearing the Word proclaimed, praying, communing with the Lord around His table, and fellowshiping with Christians, we find the encouragement and spiritual refreshment necessary to brave the attacks and challenges of a hostile environment once again. No wonder the Psalmist said, "I was glad when they said unto me, Let us go into the house of the Lord."

Have you ever said, "I just don't get anything out of the worship service"? What are you putting into it? If you do not see worship as a sublime privilege and joy, maybe you should re-evaluate your status. Have you embraced sin and ceased to be an alien in a world of sin? Are you now at home in sin?

Prayer thoughts: Ask God for strength to help you travel the paths of righteousness. Pray for a deeper appreciation of worship services through a deeper involvement in the things of God. Pray that you might have the opportunity to share your faith and love for Christ today.

—Mark McGilvrey

Bringing the Runner Home

"Be strong and of good courage, and do it: fear not, nor be dismayed: for the Lord God, even my God, will be with thee; he will not fail thee, nor forsake thee; until thou hast finished all the work . . . of the Lord" (1 Chronicles 28:20).

Read Acts 20:24; Luke 14:28-30; John 4:34.

"In the spring a young man's fancy turns to . . ." That's right, baseball, much to his girl's dismay! When you think of it, though, baseball is somewhat similar to the game of life. Let's make a few comparisons.

In a ball game and in life it's the teamwork that's important. Oh, there will be a star player—a strike-out artist or home-run king—but he can't win the ball game by himself. In life, it takes all kinds of people, doing different tasks, each one important. No one can make it alone.

Just as in a ball game, life's Coach is extremely important. He knows the score and you have to listen to Him, get your directions from Him, and look to Him for your next move. Remember, He has coached many players before you, and His team always wins!

What counts most in a ball game—the number of strikeouts a pitcher has? the hits registered on the scoreboard? the number of double plays completed by the team? No. It's the runs that cross the plate that decide the winning team. It's great when a player leads off the inning with a triple, but what good is it, if he's still on third base at the end of the inning?

What are we getting at? It's easy to start a job,

isn't it? We've got big plans! We're all excited about it! We can't wait to begin! Then, about halfway through the job, what happens? We lose our enthusiasm, our vision, our interest, and the job never gets done.

> It's not the starting of a job
> That makes some people frown,
> But it's the ending of the task
> That really gets them down.

What a thrill it is to see a job through from start to finish. Perhaps you've been on the planning committee and have followed the project all the way through to the actual event. What a sense of accomplishment you feel!

If you're looking for that thrill, that feeling of accomplishment, that excitement of completion, try witnessing to some of your friends. When you follow through and see that friend come to Christ you will experience the greatest thrill of all. You will be getting the "run across the plate." That's what counts.

Prayer thoughts: Ask God today to help you finish what you start. Pray that He will give you the strength and determination to witness to your friends.
—Donna Goodrich

Ambassador to the World

"I pray not that thou shouldest take them from the world, but that thou shouldest keep them from the evil one. . . . As thou didst send me into the world, even so sent I them into the world" (John 17:15, 18, A.S.V.).

Read John 17:14-18; 2 Corinthians 5:18-20.

It's amazing how many ways the devil finds to lead us off the one way! For instance, I was really uptight about being polluted by the evil, the apathy, the materialism, the pressures I saw around me every day. It really kept me busy trying to avoid them. The list of places I couldn't go, things I wouldn't do, and people I shouldn't get too friendly with was growing by leaps and bounds. After all, I thought, getting involved with these things could really wreck my witness to others.

Then all of a sudden I realized I didn't *have* a witness! Not a positive one, anyway, and who'd be interested in a lifetime list of no-no's? My hands were so busily occupied lifting my shirttail out of the mud that I couldn't reach out to help pull anyone else out!

You see how Satan gets us, both coming and going? I know God wants us to stay unpolluted by the corruption in the world. So I had been doing everything I could to avoid the temptations I thought would weaken me. And I ended up falling into the sin-trap of being holier-than-thou! The right road lies somewhere in the middle, but so far I haven't done too good a job of navigating. Guess I need to let the Holy Spirit have the controls. He knows what's best for me.

God doesn't want us to be like the world, but He doesn't want us to abandon it, either, shutting ourselves into some suburban monastery. We're supposed to be His ambassadors, His representatives in the world. We're supposed to bring our friends to God so they can become His friends through Christ. A foreign ambassador doesn't spend all his time closeted in the embassy, refusing to associate with the citizens of his host country. No, he's the official representative of his chief of state, and his duty is to keep informed of the attitudes in the host country and carry out the policies of his own government. He can't do this by isolating himself from everyone outside his own party!

An ambassador is *in* a foreign country—living there, getting to know the people, working to improve relations with them, speaking and acting for his chief of state—but he's not *of* that country. He's still a loyal citizen of his own nation. That's what Christians are supposed to be too. And that includes me.

Prayer thoughts: Lord, help me be an effective ambassador to the world and a worthy representative of You. Keep me free from the evil in the world, but don't let me forget those caught in Satan's trap. They need You, and I'm Your representative to them. Amen.

—Donna McQuilkin

Does Love Mean Yes or No?

"And the Lord God said, It is not good that the man should be alone; I will make him an help meet for him. . . . Therefore shall a man leave his father and his mother, and shall cleave unto his wife: and they shall be one flesh. And they were both naked, the man and his wife, and were not ashamed" (Genesis 2:18, 24, 25).

Check into Hebrews 13:4, too.

"Don't be ashamed to be what God was not ashamed to make," advises Dr. Robert Burns, marriage counselor to thousands. Dr. Burns is correct. Our sexuality is a gift of God, and sex is nothing to be ashamed of.

Why, then, has something God-given and beautiful become the subject for sleazy paperbacks, sensational movies, and slick magazines?

It is the same old story: Satan has taken something good and beautiful and twisted it into something cheap and tawdry. This is the technique Satan tried on Jesus by asking Him to turn the stones into bread.

Satan was asking Him to make a bad use of a good desire. He tempts us with this same approach. Sex is a good desire, and is one of God's precious gifts. But, as with all God's gifts, it must be used within God's purpose.

God has indicated that we are to bestow this precious gift on one chosen person, not hand it out indiscriminately like so much penny candy.

Another important fact: sex is something we *are,* not something we *do.* Sex involves our whole person and being, and cannot be isolated to a few minutes in the back seat of a car.

The young man whispers, "If you love me you will . . ." He is thinking of what he wants to do. But she answers, "If you love me, you won't . . ." She is thinking of what kind of person she is.

Does her refusal mean she is a "dead fish," and has no feeling or emotion? Does his urging reflect God's will for the two of them? What decision should they make in light of God's purpose for their lives?

Prayer thoughts: Open up to God your deepest feelings about the opposite sex, and tell Him any problems you may be having. Ask for His help in making your decisions. Begin a regular practice of praying that God will lead you to the kind of person He would have you be with.

—Rod Huron

Getting Along With My Parents

"Children, obey your parents in the Lord: for this is right. Honour thy father and mother; which is the first commandment with promise" (Ephesians 6:1, 2).

Read 1 John 4:7-12; Ephesians 6:1-4.

Lord, help me to *obey* my parents, to do willingly that which they ask of me. Help me to accept the limits that they set for me. Lord, help me to obey my parents.

Lord, help me to *honor* my parents. Help me to respect their opinions and accept their advice. Before I chalk up that advice as old-fashioned and stuffy, help me to remember that they have lived longer than I have, and they have surely learned from the living. They have "been there." Help me to realize that there are some things that one can learn only through experience and maturity. Lord, help me to honor my parents.

Lord, help me to *understand* my parents. Help me to realize why they speak and act the way they do. Help me to appreciate their labor that I may have a home to live in, clothes to wear, and food to eat. Help me to appreciate their weariness at the end of the day, the responsibility that weighs heavily on their shoulders. Lord, help me to understand my parents.

Lord, help me to *love* my parents. Even in the rough moments when things go wrong between us, help me to truly love. Help me to show my love in my attitude, my words, my actions. Help me to say, "I'm sorry"; to say, "Hey, thanks!" Help me to shoulder a few responsibilities; to help a little here and there even when I am not asked. Love is a feeling, but love is also action. Lord, help me to love my parents.

Prayer thoughts: Use the above meditation to formulate your own prayer to the Father concerning your parents and your attitude toward them. Don't be afraid to discuss specifics with the Lord. He prefers specifics to generalities anyway.

—Ruth Odor

Playing by the Rules

"There is a way which seemeth right unto a man, but the end thereof are the ways of death" (Proverbs 14:12).

Additional Scriptures: Psalm 111:7-10; Luke 16:15-17; 1 Timothy 6:11-16.

Picture a major league baseball player at bat. It's the last half of the ninth inning. The score is tied, and this is the deciding game of the world series. The pitcher winds up and lets loose with a fast ball. The batter takes off his batting helmet, catches the ball inside it, throws the ball up in the air a little, takes a powerful swing at the ball, and sends it soaring out of the park.

Imagine a professional basketball player in an important tie game. With one minute on the clock and the other team stalling for the last shot, he runs up to the man with the ball, socks him in the mouth with a blow that sends him flying, and grabs the ball to get that last shot.

Here's a pro football player in the super bowl in the last few seconds of a close game. He rushes out of the huddle, grabs the ball, and runs for a touchdown before his startled teammates or opponents can even form their lines. Would these players be likely candidates for the best player of the year award?

Athletes know there are rules that they do not dare break if they want to win the game. Any violation of the rules of play will result in a loss or penalty. The officials are constantly watching and will not permit the rules to be violated without exercising their authority and putting the proper penalty into effect.

It's the same way in the game of life. God has set down certain rules for man to live by, and He constantly watches to make sure that His rules are followed. The only difference is that God does not call the action to a halt each time a player violates a rule, but waits until the game is over and calls all the penalties at one time. All of the violations of His commandments are evident to God. Wicked men and women are not getting away with anything. There is no way to ignore God's rules in life and win the ultimate victory. In the game of life, it is not just how you play the game that counts, it is important whether you win or lose. Only through following Christ every day can life end in victory.

Prayer thoughts: Pray for strength to resist temptations to violate God's rules for living. Pray for those who are deceived, thinking that they can fool God and make up the rules as they go along. Thank God for Christ who played a perfect game of life and gives us His reward if we faithfully follow His teachings. Thank God for giving us the rule book, the Bible. Pray that through the help of Christ you might find the way to victorious Christian living and open that way to others who have not yet discovered it.

—Mark McGilvrey

What's Wrong With Alcohol?

"See then that ye walk circumspectly, not as fools, but as wise, redeeming the time, because the days are evil. Wherefore be ye not unwise, but understanding what the will of the Lord is. And be not drunk with wine, wherein is excess; but be filled with the Spirit" (Ephesians 5:15-18).

Check into Proverbs 20:1; 23:29-35, too.

So reads the ad from the neighborhood wine-making store. Make it yourself! And naturally, drink it!

What's wrong with alcohol? Nothing.

Alcohol makes a good solvent, is a fair antiseptic, can be burned as fuel, and is a good base for cough syrups and some beauty aids.

What is it?

AL·CO·HOL *noun* A volatile, inflammable, colorless liquid of penetrating odor, and burning taste, C_2H_5OH, one of the products of the distillation of fermented grains, fruit juices, and starches.

What is there about it that makes it so appealing? Teens don't have the craving the alcoholic has, nor do they very often drink themselves blind drunk just to "forget my troubles."

Isn't there another reason teens drink? What do you think it is? Isn't it usually the desire to go along with what everybody else is doing, to be popular and have a lot of friends and not stand out like a "square"?

Isn't this the real reason teens drink? Alcohol doesn't taste all that good, does it? And the smell is something else!

Prayer thoughts: Tell Jesus how you feel about drinking. Go over in your mind the people you know who drink and bring their names before God and tell Him why you think they drink. Explain to Him how people in your school feel about drinking, and ask Him to help you make the right decision whether to drink or not.

—Rod Huron

God's Authority Figures

"Honour all men. Love the brotherhood. Fear God. Honour the king" (1 Peter 2:17).

Read Romans 12:10; 13:1-5.

That brief verse from 1 Peter is deceptively simple; it holds a lot of meaning and makes some pretty stiff demands on us! It's really a summary of some of the most important principles Jesus taught for right living.

Sometimes it amazes me that Peter could write that last line, "Honour the king," when I think of who the king was and what he did to the church. It brings home the fact that Peter had to be writing under the influence of the Holy Spirit.

Nero was the emperor of Rome. When a great fire broke out and destroyed much of the city, Nero was suspected of having set it so he could build a new palace for himself in place of the old (something like setting fire to the house to collect the insurance!). In order to divert the blame from himself, Nero took advantage of the suspicion already held against the Christians and blamed them for it. After all, they taught that the world was going to end by fire! Nero brought many Christians to trial and tortured them to death. Yet Peter said to honour the king!

That gives us something to think about, in this day when respect for authority and government seems hard to come by. If Christians then were expected to show respect and honor for the king and try their best to obey the laws and live peacefully under Roman rule, it shouldn't be so hard for us! The apostles were well aware of the exceptions, but they knew that, in general, rulers punish the evil and preserve the good in society. The concept of civil government comes from God, and even Pilate ruled by God's authority (John 19:11). In a time when civil disobedience is "in," this is a hard saying!

It seems reasonable that God expects us to carry this principle of respect for authority down into the community, the school, the church, and the home. Trouble is, there are lots of people who claim to be authorities who really aren't. Teachers sometimes take advantage of their position in the classroom to sound off about things they really aren't qualified to talk about—not with authority, anyway. Oh, I know they still deserve respect for their position, but I have to remember to weigh what they say against what I believe and know by faith to be the truth of God's Word. After all, that's the only *real* authority!

Prayer thoughts: Lord, guide those in authority in my life so they can guide me with wisdom and in truth. Help me to remember that respect is due to those in authority, whether I always agree with them or not. In Jesus' name, amen.

—Donna McQuilkin

Dropouts From God

"Can any hide himself in secret places that I shall not see him? saith the Lord. Do not I fill heaven and earth? saith the Lord" (Jeremiah 23:24).

Additional Scriptures: 1 Kings 8:27; Psalm 139:3-10; Acts 17:23-31.

Dropping out is the popular thing to do. If school is too much work or too confining, students simply drop out. If society in general seems to cause more problems than a person can bear, he drops out by traveling the hippie way of life or by the more sophisticated route of suicide. If the political scene looks unfavorable to one's pet ideals, he drops out by joining the radical revolutionary group in vogue.

If it looks as though the draft board may call your magic number soon, the thing to do is to drop out by joining the war protest movement. If a marriage becomes a strain and requires some honest effort by both parties, drop out through divorce, and jump on the free-love bandwagon. If working regularly becomes a drag, drop out and hallucinate. If the home becomes a battlefield where parents and teens fight, run off and live in the streets.

With the dropout disease so common today, it is not surprising that many people, young and old alike, are afflicted with it when they are faced with the commandments of God. When people see the demands for righteous living contained in God's Word, they begin to develop the symptoms of the dropout disease. They deny that the Bible is the Word of God. They try to find mistakes in the Bible hoping that these demands for righteous living will be mistakes as well. They deny punishment for the wicked and reward for the righteous. They look for faults in the lives of those who claim to be living for God in an effort to elevate themselves by standing on others. They try to concoct philosophies that will take the place of God and at the same time numb the pain of a guilty conscience by denying the truth of God's plan.

Some dropouts from God actually try to hide from God by denying His existence. Many of these dropouts succeed in deceiving themselves into thinking that they have successfully gotten away from God, but God's questions in Jeremiah quickly melt these delusions. "Can any hide himself in secret places that I shall not see him? Do not I fill heaven and earth?"

Have you been hiding from God, denying His Word, trying to deceive yourself? Get with it. Face reality with God.

Prayer thoughts: Pray for courage to face life's problems. Thank God for His presence wherever man may go. Pray for wisdom to show honest people the fallacy in their philosophies that leave God out. Pray for an understanding of life that will prohibit your being confused by the godless philosophies commonly advanced.

—Mark McGilvrey

You, and Your Special Gifts

"Let no man despise thy youth; but be thou an example of the believers, in word, in conversation, in charity, in spirit, in faith, in purity" (1 Timothy 4:12).

Read Jeremiah 1:6-10; 1 Peter 4:8-10.

"Let no man despise thy youth." Don't underestimate yourself or the contribution you can make to your family and to the world. Being not quite adult does not mean being second-rate. You are neither an adult nor a child, but this age called youth has certain gifts to offer that no other age has. What do you have to offer your family that no other member of the family can offer?

Youth means alive, enthusiastic, ready for action. You are ready to act and to act now! Of course, we do need to do some planning, but often adults never get their plans off the ground. They have a lot of good intentions, but no action. How about that church work you and your family have been talking about doing, that mission project? Use your enthusiasm to get some action going, now!

Another gift of yours is your way of questioning, challenging old and accepted truths. It's OK to question the truths of the Bible—they'll stand. Questions help us to get at the heart of the matter, to find the real issues.

How about your ability to dream, to envision the future? Oh, one can be too idealistic, and there can be too much dreaming and too little action, but, as the song goes, "You've got to have a dream, or how you gonna make a dream come true?"

Perhaps one of your best gifts is your ability for total commitment—commitment without reservations. In a mixed-up, war-torn world, a graduate closed her speech by saying, "And without reservations, we accept the challenge." That's what teenagers do: accept the challenge, without reservations, no ifs, ands, or buts. You can give yourself to a friend, a hero, a cause, a talent, a work.

Only one cause is really worthy of total commitment, and that is the cause of the Man of Galilee. That's exactly what He asks, total commitment, a kind of reckless daring, casting all else aside, and going His way and doing His will.

"Let no man despise thy youth; but be thou an example of the believers."

Prayer thoughts: Thank God for the special gifts that are yours now just because you are a teen-ager. Ask Him to show you how to use those gifts for Him.

—Ruth Odor

A Chosen Generation

"But ye are a chosen generation, a royal priesthood, an holy nation, a peculiar people; that ye should shew forth the praises of him who hath called you out of darkness into his marvellous light" (1 Peter 2:9).

Read Philippians 4:13; Matthew 28:18-20.

A chosen generation! What better way can we describe the youth of today? You are better educated than youth have ever been. You have more influence, more spending money, more freedom to do as you please than any youth in history. Eighteen-year-olds can now vote; in many states you can hold public office; you are experienced drivers of motor vehicles.

Today's chosen generation is searching. This is the generation of the "Jesus people." It is the "now" thing to be a Christian. A chosen generation, indeed! But chosen for what?

It happened in Moscow. A Japanese newspaper correspondent returned to the Orient to relate his eyewitness account of a youth demonstration staged in Red Square. Thousands of Communist youth had paraded before the reviewing stand shouting, "We are hungry and ragged, but we're changing the world."

This is the work cut out for your generation— changing the world! This was the goal of the early church. In spite of beatings, stoning, and imprisonment, three thousand souls were added to the church, then five thousand. Soon the world was "turned upside down."

You have the truth that can change the world. It may take some sacrifice on your part, but so what? The Communist youth were willing to sacrifice for something in which they believed. Isn't it far greater to sacrifice for Someone in whom you believe?

Changing the world is a big undertaking, but you have a big God. Don't become overwhelmed by looking at the tremendous task before you. Simply start with yourself. Ask God to change you to become an effective witness for Him. Then proceed to the friend closest to you. Witness to him. Show by your life what God can do when you let Him. Let your family see Christ in you. "Each one win one, till the work is done."

"Ye are a chosen generation"—for what? to change the world for Christ.

Prayer thoughts: Ask God today to help you to become part of the chosen generation that can change the world.

—Donna Goodrich

Welcome to the Land of the Living

"Jesus said unto her, I am the resurrection, and the life: he that believeth in me, though he were dead, yet shall he live: and whosoever liveth and believeth in me shall never die. Believest thou this?" (John 11:25, 26).

A psychiatrist wanted to talk with dying patients about their feelings and views concerning death. She went to one of the largest hospitals in Chicago and went to the nurse or doctor in charge of each floor. To her astonishment, there were no dying patients in the hospital. Each time she was told, "There are none."

Every day, however, several patients in that hospital died. The doctors and nurses refused to admit that any of their patients were dying. To talk of the patients' death reminded the hospital staff that they too would someday die.

We don't like to think about death, let alone talk about it. It reminds us of our great limitation. We are mortal, and all mortals must eventually die. We get superinvolved in the humdrum business of everyday life to the extent that we repress all thoughts of dying.

Whether we think or talk about death or not, it still remains, "It is appointed unto men once to die" (Hebrews 9:27). To some death comes quickly, as a thief in the night. It knows no age limits. Teenagers are not isolated from the reality of death.

Man, what a hassle! I don't want to die!

Again, up walks Jesus and announces triumphantly, "I am the resurrection, and the life: he that believeth in me shall never die." Jesus was looking down the road to the life to come.

The last words of Edward the Confessor were: "Weep not, I shall not die; and as I leave the land of the dying I trust to see the blessings of the Lord in the land of the living." We, with limited vision, call this world the land of the living; but it would be more correct to call it the land of the dying. Through Jesus Christ we know that when death comes we do not pass out of the land of the living, but into it. Through Jesus Christ we know we are journeying, not to the sunset, but to the sunrise.

Through powerful faith, Paul could shout, "For me to live is Christ, and to die is gain." The last enemy has been defeated. Death is dead, and life begins to live. There is hope. In Jesus we can share the Indian's confidence in the Great Father and say, "Today is a good day to die."

Have a happy forever.

Words from the Word: Philippians 1:21-23; Romans 6:7-10; 1 Corinthians 15:20-22.

Prayer thoughts: Think about the reality of death. Thank God that you are part of the forever family. P.T.L.

—Tom Smith

ALLEN ROAD MISSIONARY CHURCH
16388 ALLEN ROAD
NORTH OF PENNSYLVANIA RD.
TAYLOR. MICHIGAN 48180